How to Trade Options:

A Beginner's Guide to Investing and Making Profit with Options Trading

Warren Ray Benjamin

Table of Contents

Introduction

Welcome to How to Trade Options: A Beginner's Guide. In this book, we'll introduce you to the exciting and challenging world of options. While options involve higher risk-taking than normal stock market investing, they are also more interesting and exciting, with a huge potential upside. Some of the topics we'll be discussing in this book include:

- Learning what options are and the entire industry lingo.
- Find out the top reasons to trade options.
- Answer the question: Is trading options really for you?
- Learn to avoid common mistakes made by beginners.
- Find out the best strategies for beginners in the Markets.

And much more!

By the time you finish this book, you should understand how options work, how and where to trade them, and be able to converse like an expert. You'll also know the strategies used by the pros to trade options and profit handsomely and how to apply them yourself.

Options' trading is not for everyone. Before you jump in, you should study options carefully, so you know what you're getting into. While options can help you gain profits quickly as compared to normal stock trading which is a long-term endeavor, there is heightened risk.

- Understand your risk profile: If you are not a risk taker and see bonds and mutual funds as places where you want to put your money, options might be too risky for you. However, you should learn about them first. There are options...when it comes to options that can help reduce risk, so there may be a place for you in the space. It is best to learn it firsthand to get a better idea of what your profile is and how you prefer to trade.

- Understand your financial situation: Before jumping into any new investment program, make sure you have a clear picture of where you stand financially. You should know where you are at for income, credit card debts, taxes, other loans, and obligations. Have a clear idea of how much capital you can really afford to lose.

- Be an analyst, not a careless risk taker: Options require a deeper understanding of the markets than regular stock trading does. The excitement that arises from the possibility of fast and large profits can overwhelm some people, leading to excessive risk-taking. Be aware of this and put the time in to do analysis rather than looking only for a fast buck.

- Don't invest money you aren't willing to lose. Before engaging in options trading, make sure you're not gambling with money you need for essentials.

Please note that while we're bullish on options trading, all trading and investment activity carries with it some risk. If done correctly, a trader can earn substantial profits from their activities; however, some traders will be at risk of losing substantial amounts of money. No guarantees can be made, and the topics discussed in this book are presented for informational and educational purposes only and are not to be taken as actual financial advice. The best teacher yet experiences and once you know the basics, it is time to get your feet wet and apply what you have learned!

Chapter 1: Options Contracts: The Basics

In this chapter, we will introduce the concept of options contracts and how they are used in the stock market. In our introductory discussion, we will be focusing on the most basic way to get involved in options, which involves buying options contracts based on bets you make on whether future stock prices will rise or fall. Later we will see that you can also write or sell options contracts and that the contracts themselves are traded on the markets.

What is an Options Contract?

An options contract sounds fancy but it's a pretty simple concept.

- It's a contract. That means it's a legal agreement between a buyer and a seller.
- It gives the purchaser of the contract the opportunity to purchase or dispose of an asset with a fixed amount.
- The purchase is optional – so the buyer of the contract does not have to buy or sell the asset.
- The contract has an expiration date, so the purchaser – if they choose to exercise their right – must make the trade on or before the expiration date.
- The purchaser of the contract pays a non-refundable fee for the contract.

While the focus of this book is on options contracts related to the stock market, there are options contracts that take place in all aspects of daily life including real estate and speculation. A simple example illustrates the concept of an options contract.

Suppose you are itching to buy a BMW and you've decided the model you want must be silver. You drop by a local dealer and it turns out they don't have a silver model in stock. The dealer claims he can get you one by the end of the month. You say you'll take the car if the dealer can get it by the last day of the month and he'll sell it to you for $67,500. He agrees and requires you to put a $3,000 deposit on the car.

If the last day of the month arrives and the dealer hasn't produced the car, then you're freed from the contract and get your money back. In the event he does produce the car at any date before the end of the month, you have the option to buy it or not. If you really wanted the car you can buy it, but of course, you can't be forced to buy the car, and maybe you've changed your mind in the interim.

The right is there but not the obligation to purchase, in short, no pressure if you decided not to push through with the purchase of the car. If you decide to let the opportunity pass, however, since the dealer met his end of the bargain and produced the car, you lose the $3,000 deposit.

In this case, the dealer, who plays the role of the writer of the contract, *has the obligation to follow through with the sale* based upon the agreed upon price.

Suppose that when the car arrives at the dealership, BMW announces it will no longer make silver cars. As a result, prices of new silver BMWs that were the last ones to roll off the assembly line, skyrocket. Other dealers are selling their silver BMWs for $100,000. However, since this dealer entered into an options contract with you, he must sell the car to you for the pre-agreed price of $67,500. You decide to get the car and drive away smiling, knowing that you saved $32,500 and that you could sell it at a profit if you wanted to.

The situation here is capturing the essence of options contracts, even if you've never thought of haggling with a car dealer in those terms.

An option is in a sense a kind of bet. In the example of the car, the bet is that the dealer can produce the exact car you want within the specified time period and at the agreed upon price. The dealer is betting too. His bet is that the pre-agreed to price is a good one for him. Of course, if BMW stops making silver cars, then he's made the wrong bet.

It can work the other way too. Let's say that instead of BMW deciding not to make silver cars anymore when your car is being driven onto the lot, another car crashes into it. Now your silver BMW has a small dent on the rear bumper with some scratches. As a result, the car has immediately declined in value. But if you want the car, since you've agreed to the options contract, you must pay $67,500, even though with the dent it's only really worth $55,000. You can walk away and lose your $3,000 or pay what is now a premium price on a damaged car.

Another example that is commonly used to explain options contracts is the purchase of a home to be built by a developer under the agreement that certain conditions are met. The buyer will be required to put a non-refundable down payment or deposit on the home. Let's say that the developer agrees to build them the home for $300,000 provided that a new school is built within 5 miles of the development within one year. So, the contract expires within a year. At any time during the year, the buyer has the option to go forward with the construction of the home for $300,000 if the school is built. The developer has agreed to the price no matter what. So if the housing market in general and the construction of the school, in particular, drive up demand for housing in the area, and the developer is selling new homes that are now priced at $500,000, he has to sell this home for $300,000 because that was the price agreed to when the contract was signed. The home buyer got what they wanted, being within 5 miles of the new school with the home price fixed at $300,000. The developer was assured of the sale but missed out on the unknown, which was the skyrocketing price that occurred as a result of increased demand. On the other hand, if the school isn't built and the buyers don't exercise their option to buy the house before the contract expires at one year, the developer can pocket the $20,000 cash.

What is an options contract on the stock market?

An options contract on the stock market is somewhat analogous to the fictitious situation we just described with the car. In the case of the car, we saw that unforeseen events can make the bet made by the buyer and the car dealer profitable or not. The same thing happens in the stock market. Of course in the case of the car, the buyer is simply hoping to get the car they want at what they perceive to be a bargain price, although if BMW really stopped making silver cars, they might sell it to a third party and then get a white one from the dealer. However, in most cases, the buyer wants the car. That isn't the case when it comes to options with stocks.

On the stock market, we are betting on the future price itself, and the shares of stock will be bought or sold at a profit if things work out. The key point is the buyer of the options contract is not hoping to acquire the shares and hold them for a long time period like a traditional investor. Instead, you're hoping to make a bet on the price of the stock, secure that price, and then be able to trade the shares on that price no matter what happens on the actual markets. We will illustrate this with an example.

CALL Options

A call is a type of option contract that provides the option to purchase an asset at the agreed upon amount at the designated time or deadline. The reason you would do this is if you felt that the price of a given stock would increase in price over the specified time period. Let's illustrate with an example.

Suppose that Acme Communications makes cutting edge smartphones. The rumors are that they will announce a new smartphone in the next three weeks that is going to take the market by storm, with customers lined out the door to make preorders.

The current price that Acme Communications is trading at is $44.25 a share. The current pricing of an asset is termed as the *spot price*. Put another way, the spot price is the actual amount that you would be paying for the shares as you would buy it from the stock market right now.

Nobody really knows if the stock price will go up when the announcement is made, or if the announcement will even be made. But you've done your research and are reasonably confident these events will take place. You also have to estimate how much the shares will go up and based on your research you think it's going to shoot up to $65 a share by the end of the month.

You enter into an options contract for 100 shares at $1 per share. You pay this fee to the brokerage that is writing the options contract. In total, for 100 shares you pay $100.

The price that is paid for an options contract is $100. This price is called the *premium*.

You don't get the premium back. It's a fee that you pay no matter what. If you make a profit, then it's all good. But if your bet is wrong, then you'll lose the premium. For the buyer of an options contract, the premium is their risk.

You'll want to set a price that you think is going to be lower than the level to which the price per share will rise. The price that you agree to is called the *strike price*. For this contract, you set your strike price at $50.

Remember, exercising your right to buy the shares is optional. You'll only buy the shares if the price goes high enough that you'll make a profit on the trade. If the shares never go above $50, say they reach $48, you are not obligated to buy them. And why would you? As part of the contract deal, you'd be required to buy them at $50.

We'll say that the contract is entered on the 1st of August, and the deadline is the third Friday in August. If the price goes higher than your strike price during that time, you can exercise your option.

Let's say that as the deadline approaches, things go basically as you planned. Acme Communications announces its new phone, and the stock starts climbing. The stock price on the actual market (the spot price) goes up to $60.

Now the seller is required to sell you the shares at $50 a share. You buy the shares, and then you can immediately dispose of these at a quality or optimal amount, or $60 a share. You make a profit of $10 a share, not taking into account any commissions or fees.

The Call Seller

The call seller who enters into the options contract with the buyer is obligated to sell the shares to the buyer of the options contract at the strike price. If the contract sets the strike price at $50 a share for 100 shares, the seller must sell the stock at that price even if the market price goes up to any higher price, such as $70 a share. The call seller keeps the premium. So, if the buyer doesn't exercise their option, the call seller still gets the money from the premium.

Derivative Contracts

You probably heard about derivatives or derivative contracts during the 2008 financial crisis. While they can be designed in complex ways, the concept of a derivative contract is pretty simple. What this means is that the contract is based on some underlying asset. For an options contract, the asset is the stock that you agree to buy or sell. The contracts themselves can and are bought and sold. That is why you may have heard about people trading in derivatives. The stock that is the subject of an options contract is called the *underlying*.

So, if you buy an options contract using the Apple stock price as a basis, the term "underlying" would be applicable to the stock from Apple.

Profits from the Call

Keep in mind the brokerage may have some additional fees. However, using our numbers remember that we paid a premium of $1 per share, and the strike price was $50. Computing for profit is one of the basics when it comes to trading. It is where profits are determined and forecasted for future options to buy or sell.

The profit per share was:

Profit = $60 − ($50 + $1) = $9 per share

The contract was for 100 shares, so the total profit would be $90.

What happens if the strike price isn't reached?

The strike price is the fundamental piece of information you need to keep in mind when trading options. If the strike price isn't reached, then the option will simply expire and be worthless. The difference between the current market price or spot price and the strike price is a measure of the profit per share that you will make.

For example, $100 is the price of the stock, and the strike price is $75, then the profit (disregarding fees) will be $25. If the strike price was $95, then the profit per share would only be $5. While the pay off from a strike price that is closer to the actual market price is smaller, it's more likely to pay off than a strike price that predicts a big move.

Why purchase a call option

The reason that you purchase an options contract is to reduce your risk. When you buy an options contract, the only money you're putting at risk is the premium. In the case of our hypothetical example, that is $100. If the stock doesn't surpass the strike price, you can simply walk away from the deal and only lose the $100.

You could, of course, buy the stocks outright and hope to profit. To buy 100 shares, you'll have to invest substantially more money:

100 x $44.25 = $4,425.

If the stock goes up value, then you'll make some money. However, suppose that your hunch about the markets was wrong. Maybe Acme Communications, rather than announcing a new phone that will be in high demand, instead reveals that their next phone will be delayed for a year.

If you decide to unload the stocks you bought for $4,425, you will only get $4,000, and you'll have lost $425.

On the other hand, you can see how you reduced your risk by purchasing a call option. In that case, you won't exercise your right to buy the stock and only lose the premium. Your total loss would be $100.

The Flexibility of Options

In normal stock trading, you're betting on one direction, that the value of the stock will go up with time. And you're battling the opposite, hoping to avoid losses if the stock declines.

Options open the door to making a profit when stocks decline in value. Of course, it depends on being able to make the right call, but if you bet on a stock losing value and you're right, you can make substantial profits. Timing and the size of your trade will be important too, and you'll have to stay focused on the strike price and the current market price of the underlying.

Put Options

A call option is the option to buy a stock if it reaches the strike price. Now let's look at the opposite situation. A *put* is an option contract where you get the right but not the obligation to *sell* a stock before the contract expires. Returning to our previous example, suppose that Acme Communications looks to be heading to bad times and the stock is trading at $44.25 a share. Your bet is that it's going to decrease to at least $35 a share, so you buy a put option with a strike price of $35 a share. If your bet that the stock will decline in value and you're correct, let's say it drops to $30 a share, then you can make a $5 per share profit on the sale. If the stock meets the strike price, the seller of the put is obligated to purchase the stock at that price. In other words, even though the stock has dropped in value to

$30 a share on the market, they must buy the shares from you at $35 a share.

Let's suppose that instead it only drops to $38 a share. In this case, you don't have to sell and simply walk away from the deal having paid the premium. So once again, as was the case with a call option, the premium is really the only money that you risk as to the buyer.

The seller of a put option *must* buy the stock from you at the strike price if you exercise your option. If the strike price is $35 but for some reason, the stock crashes to $1, the seller of the put must buy the shares from you at $35.

Why Buy a Put Option?

The answer is simple – when you buy stocks the usual way, you don't make any money from the declining values of stocks. You lose money. With a put option, it gives you the possibility of betting on the stock losing value.

Summary: Buyers of Options

The buyer of an options contract:

- Must pay the premium. This is non-refundable, so the premium is the minimum amount of capital you invest and is the amount you risk.
- You are not obligated to buy or sell any stock even when the deadline arrives.
- You have purchased the right to buy or sell the stock.
- If you buy a call, then you have the option to purchase the expiry of the agreement. If you buy a put, you have the option to sell the stock when the expiry arrives. The option to sell only falls in instances when there is a marked difference between the market price and your own strike price; with the market price being too low.

Summary: Sellers of Calls and Puts

Later we'll see that you may want to sell options and there are good reasons for doing so. Right now, we'll just summarize the general principles.

- The seller of an options contract will keep the premium no matter what. So, if the buyer doesn't exercise their option, you keep the premium as profit.

- If the buyer of a call option exercises their option to buy the stock, you must sell it to them at the strike price. So, if the strike price is $40 but the current market price is $65, you are missing out on a large profit per share. However, as we'll see later this can still be profitable.

- If the buyer exercises their right on a put contract, you must buy the stock from them at the deadline.

Number of Shares

The number of shares in one options contract is 100 shares. Typically, traders will trade multiple contracts. To you'll get the profit per share and then calculate total profit as (profit per share * 100 shares * # of contracts).

Now let's get familiar with the industry jargon so you can have a better understanding of what is going on when you start trading.

Chapter 2: Options Trading Jargon

Every industry has its own specialized lingo, and options trading is no exception. Let's give a quick overview that will help you understand what is being discussed when reading about options and help you navigate the markets effectively.

Ask

The price that a seller is asking for security or put another way the smallest price a seller is willing to accept to sell it.

Assignment

When the buyer of an options contract exercises their option, a notice is sent to the seller. The seller is then obligated to dispose of (in the case of a call) or purchase (in the case of a put) stocks at the strike price.

At the Money

This means that the current market price is equal to the strike price.

Bid Price

This term refers to the optimum amount that a dealer is willing to shell out for the security.

Break Even Point

When neither a profit nor loss has been realized.

Call

Summarizing what was introduced in the last chapter, the buyer of a call option has the right to buy 100 shares of a stock at the strike price at any time before the options contract expires. This is an option, so the buyer does not have to buy the shares. The seller of a call contract must buy the shares under any circumstances up to the expiration of the contract if the buyer exercises their right before the contract expires.

Commission

A fee charged by a brokerage firm to execute an option order on an exchange.

Delta

If the underlying stock changes by a point in value, the delta is the change in the value of the option.

Early Exercise

If an options contract is exercised before the expiration date, it is said to be early.

Exercise

The buyer of the option exercises their right to buy stock for a call or sell the stock for a put.

Expiration Date

Options contracts expire on the third Friday of every month. When you see an option quote such as:

JUN 70

That means that the option expires on the third Friday in June, with a strike price of $70.

In the Money (Call)

This refers to the occurrence of when the current market price exceeds the strike price. This is the gross profit per share (not including premium and other fees).

In the Money (Put)

For a put contract, it is in-the-money when the current stock price is less than the strike price.

Index Options

An index option doesn't have individual stocks as the underlying. Instead the underlying is an index like the NASDAQ. An index option can't be exercised until the expiry date.

Intrinsic Value

An apt example would be – if the current price is at $10, then the market price is at $20, the intrinsic value would be $10. If the current price were $25, the intrinsic value would be $15.

LEAP
A LEAP is a long-term equity anticipation security. Basically, these are long term options contracts. LEAP contracts can last as long as three years. LEAPS are generally more expensive than most options, because of the longtime value which gives them more time to be "in the money."

Legs
A leg is one part of a position when there are two or more options or positions in the underlying stock.

Long
Long means ownership when it is held in your account. You can belong on a stock or an option.

Margin Requirement
If you are selling options, you will be required to deposit some cash with the brokerage to cover

your positions. In other words, it is cash in your account with the brokerage to buy or sell shares as required by your obligations in the options contract.

Option Chain

An option chain is something you'll look at when viewing available options online. It's basically a table for the options available for a given underlying stock. For given expiration date, the option chain will include all puts and calls, and strike prices that are available.

Out-of-the-Money

This is the amount that a stock price is below the strike price for a call, or above the strike price for a put. If your price $50 but the market is $40, you're "out of the money" $10. If your strike price for a put is $50, but the market price is $60, you're out of the money $10.

Premium

This is the price paid per share for an options contract. Since the contract has 100 shares, the price paid, or the total premium is 100 times the premium. The seller is able to keep the premium regardless of whether or not the buyer exercises their options.

Put

The buyer of a put option has the right to sell 100 shares at the strike price on or before the expiry date. The seller of a put option has an obligation to buy 100 shares if required by the buyer.

Roll a Long Position

Rolling a long position means to sell options and then acquire others with the same underlying stock but with different strike prices and expiration dates. We will talk a bit more about rolling options in the chapter on advanced trading strategies.

Roll a Short Position

Rolling a short position means buying to close an existing position and selling for the purposes of opening new positions with different strike prices and expiration dates "rolled out" in time.

Series

Options are grouped together in series on the markets. Options in the same series can be calls or puts, but they have the same expiration date and strike price.

Short

Selling a security that you don't actually own.

Strike Price

It is the amount per share of the agreed upon contract. If the option to buy or sell is exercised by the purchaser of an options contract, the shares must be bought or sold at the strike price. When you look at options online, the strike price is given at the end of the options symbol. For example, you might see:

00040000

The decimal point is found by moving three places from the right. So, this represents a strike price of $40. On the other hand

00005600

It would represent a strike price of $5.60.

Time Value

How long is left until an options contract expires? Generally, more time value will mean that an option is worth more when trading. The reason is that the more time until the option expires, the more chance there is for the underlying stock to beat the strike price. In the case of a call option that means going above the strike price, while in the case of a put option that means going below the strike price. What investors are looking for is enough time value for an option to be in the money.

Time Decay

Time decay is simply a measure of the decrease in the time value of an options contract.

Underlying

The underlying stock is the specific stock that the option contract is based on. This is the stock that is actually traded if the option is exercised.

Weekly

A weekly is a kind of option that expires within a week, rather than a monthly time frame. Since weekly's have a short time value, they are cheaper, but the risks involved are higher. Investors who like weekly's are hoping to capitalize on an option that tightly fits a given date coming up in the near future. Weeklies usually expire on Friday afternoons at market close. Weeklies help traders that are trying to exploit short term events for profits. For example, investors might target an earnings report or an anticipated product announcement.

Three ways to close an options contract

Now let's learn the three basic ways that you can close an options contract, now that we have some familiarity with the lingo.

- The option expires out of the money. That means that the option is worthless. You do nothing and move on. The seller of the option simply pockets the premium.

- The option expires in the money. In that case, it's up to the buyer to exercise their options. If they choose to, then the underlying stock is traded.

- The last option is to sell the option – i.e., trade it to someone else – prior to the expiration date. If you are losing money on the options contract, you can trade it and cut your losses now, rather than finding out what will happen if you hold it to the expiration date. On the other hand, if you are profiting from the option, you can sell it to get out now with profits.

Although we are spending a lot of time talking about exercising the option with the contract, options are only exercised in about 12% of trades. About 20% expire as worthless contracts. The rest are bought and sold prior to the expiration date.

Reading Options Quotes

It's important to know how to read options quotes. Some have more information in them than others because some of the associated information is implied. First, let's look at this fictitious options quote:

ACMC   AUGUST 12, 2019   120   CALL AT $2.50

- ACMC is the stock ticker. Our example is our fictitious company, Acme Communications.
- The date given is the expiration date of the option.
- 120 is the strike price, or $120.

- We're told it's a call option, or a bet the stock will increase in price.
- The final quoted price, $2.50, is the premium paid per share.

If an option is shaded in the online display, that means it's in the money. Options that are not shaded are out of the money.

Chapter 3: Strike Price

The strike price is one of the most important if not the most important thing to understand when it comes to option contracts. The strike price will determine whether the underlying stock is actually bought or sold at or before the expiration date. When evaluating any options contract, the strike price is the first thing that you should look at. It's worth reviewing the concept and how it's utilized in the actual marketplace.

The strike price will let you home in on the profits that can be made on an options contract. It's the break-even point but also gives you an idea as to your profits and losses. Of course, the seller always gets the premium no matter what.

For a call contract, the strike price is the price that must be exceeded by the current market price of the underlying equity. For example, if the strike price is $100 on a call contract, and the current market price goes to any price above $100, then the purchaser of the call can exercise their right at any time to buy the stock. Then the stock can be disposed of with a profit. Suppose that the current price rises to $130. Then you can exercise your option to buy the stock at $100 a share, and then turn around and sell it on the market for $130 a share, making a $30 profit per share before taking into account the premium and other fees that might accrue with your trades. While as the buyer of the contract you have no obligations other than paying the premium, the seller is obligated no matter what, and they must sell you the shares at $100 per share no matter how much it pains them to see the $130 per share price. Of course, there are reasons behind the curtain that will explain why they would bother entering this kind of arrangement that we will explore later.

For a put contract, the strike price likewise plays a central role, but the value of the stock relative to the strike price works in the opposite fashion. A put is a bet that the underlying equity will decrease in value by a certain amount. Hence if the stock price drops below the strike price, then the buyer can exercise their right to sell the shares at the strike price even though the market price is lower. So, if your price is $100, if the current price of the equity drops to $80, the seller obligated to buy the 100 shares per contract from you at $100 a share even though the market price is $80 per share. In this case, you've made a gross profit of $20 a share.

The value of the strike price will not only tell you profitability but give you an indication of how much the stock must move before you are able to exercise your rights. Often when the amount is smaller, you might be better off.

When you know the strike price of different options contracts, then you can evaluate which one is better for you to buy. Suppose that a stock is currently trading at $80 and you find two options put contracts. One has a strike price of $75 and the other has a strike price of $60. Further, let's suppose that both contracts expire at the same time. In the first case, the stock price in the market will need to drop just $5 before the contract becomes profitable. For the second contract, it will have to drop $20.

The potential worth of each contract per share is the difference. For the contract with the $75 strike price, that is only $5. For the second contract with the strike price of $60, the potential worth is $20, four times as much.

Determining which contract is better is a matter of analysis and taking some risk. You can't just go by face value, but you must take into consideration the expiration date together with an analysis of what the stock will actually do over that time period. It may be that it's going to be impossible for the stock to drop $20 in order to make the second contract valuable. If the expiration date comes before the stock drops that much in price, the contract will be worthless. In other words, you'd never be able to exercise your option of selling shares at strike amount. On the other hand, even though there is not much discrepancy between the strike and the market amount for the first contract, and the market price might only drop to say $70 per share, the chances of this happening before the expiration date is more likely.

Your analysis might be different if the contract with the lower strike price has a longer expiration date.

The lesson to take to heart is that a stock is more likely to move by smaller amounts over short time periods. But the higher the risk, the more the potential profits.

Chapter 4: Understanding the purchase of Options

Let's suppose that you're interested in buying shares in Acme Communications, and they are trading at $39 a share. To buy 100 shares, it would cost $3,900 plus brokerage/commission fees. For many people that is a lot of money to invest, and if you are a savvy investor, you might be more interested in purchasing options that you would be in laying out that much money per share. Keep in mind that our discussion below doesn't consider account brokerage commissions.

Suppose that instead you purchase an options contract and the price is $2.50. The premium is quoted on a per share basis, but an options contract is for 100 shares, so the total amount you will need to invest is 100 x $2.50 = $250.

Now suppose that you're bullish on the stock, and you settle on a strike price of $41. Let's say that on or before the expiration date the market price of Acme communications reaches $47.

Your gross profit per share is now $6. You've made $6 x 100 = $600. Subtracting the amount invested, not including commissions your profit is $600-$250 = $350. That's a return on investment of 140%.

If you had bought the shares, you could sell them at $47 a share for a profit of $800. While that is a bigger number in absolute terms, your return on investment would be about 21%.

Of course, depending on your financial situation, you aren't limited to purchasing one option contract. Remember that the stock was $39 a share, so if a person bought $3900 worth or 100 shares, they could have instead gone with 16 options contracts for $250 x 16 = $4,000. While the direct investor would have made their $800 profit, assuming that they sold when the price hit $47 a share, the options trader would have made

$350 x 16 = $5,600 in profit (remember for both options – not considering commissions).

The downside is the risk that the stock price won't exceed the strike price. In that case, you're out the premium. If you had purchased 16 options contracts, then you'd be out the $4,000. The person who buys the stock won't be out nearly that much money. Let's say that the stock dropped to $37 a share. If they felt it would not be going anywhere anytime soon and they should sell at a loss, the person who bought the stocks would sell for $37 x 100 = $3700 and only be out $200 from their initial investment.

Using this example, you can see how investing in options contracts has a big upside in potential profits but also a bigger risk in losses. When you are talking about trading a single contract for 100 shares, the losses don't seem like a big deal, but you can see that going for more trades means that you're going to have to have a lot more awareness of the risks.

Of course, the options trader has one big advantage that the ordinary stock investor will never have, and that is the possibility of betting on the stock decreasing in value. Let's suppose that instead of dropping to $37 a share the stock dropped by $10 to $29 a share. So, 100 shares would be worth $2,900, and our investor friend would have lost $1,000 if they sell at that point.

Now let's say that instead of a call you invest in a put contract, the same scenario you buy 16 of them at $2.50, or $250 per contract. So, your total cost is again $4,000. This time say you have a strike price of $35. Your profit is $35-$29 = $6 per share.

This time you've made $9,600 ($6 per share, x 100 shares/contract x 16 contracts). With your initial investment, you've made a profit of $5,600 on the decline in stock price while your friend is nursing their losses. Again, you made a 140% ROI.

So, we see that buying options contracts can carry bigger risks while at the same time offering the potential for bigger rewards. In addition, they also offer the possibility of reaping the rewards when a stock drops in price, something that just isn't going to be possible with normal investing in stocks.

Chapter 5: Top Reasons to Trade Options

We've seen that trading options are an activity that has its upsides and its downsides. In this chapter, we are going to look at the top reasons that you want to trade options. Keep in mind that you can personalize your portfolio and investment strategy, so it's not necessary to go "all in" when it comes to trading options. You can have options trading as one part of a diverse investment strategy. In fact, many people use options to cover risks in other parts of their overall portfolio.

1. Trading Options provides an investment opportunity with limited capital

In the last chapter, we began with an example showing that for $250, you could control 100 shares of stock that would cost someone $3,900 to buy outright. We then expanded on that and saw what kind of possibilities existed when investing larger amounts. However, if you are just starting out with investing, it's not necessary to buy more than one options contract at a time. You can invest for a relatively small amount of money depending on the stock. Trading doesn't have to be approached with an all or nothing mentality. You can start with small investments and work your way up by reinvesting your profits.

2. You can hedge your risks with index funds

Most people who invest in stocks will be investing in index funds in order to have a diversified portfolio. By utilizing options, you can hedge your risks with index funds. Index puts can help you mitigate losses if the market experiences a major downturn. Smart investors will utilize index puts so that the next recession doesn't leave them with huge losses.

3. Profit off of other losses

OK, it sounds bad when phrased that way. But as we saw in the last chapter, you can use puts to profit from downturns in stock prices. This is an opportunity that simply isn't available when doing regular stock trading.

4. Collect Premiums

In the coming chapters, we'll investigate selling options contracts. As we'll see, there are ways to profit from doing so, but no matter what, you can pocket the premiums. This is another way to earn money in an overall investment portfolio that uses diverse strategies as well as diverse investments.

5. Capitalize on outsized gains

One of the biggest benefits that come with trading options is being able to control large amounts of stock that could have a huge upside if there is a major increase in stock price by purchasing a large number of call options. Of course, being a fortune teller isn't generally a lucrative income, but you can increase your chances of success by carefully studying the markets and the companies behind the individual stocks. Look for dynamic areas where new companies could see a huge gain in the stock price over a short period. The risk is that you'll lose your premium if the strike price isn't surpassed, but if it is then you'll have a chance to score big. In the previous chapter, we showed a simple example with a return on investment of 140%, but it's even possible to get an ROI of 500% or even more.

Chapter 6: Covered Calls

In this chapter, we'll investigate a trading strategy that is a good way to get started selling options for beginners. This strategy is called covered calls. By covered, we mean that you've got an asset that you own that covers the potential sale of the underlying stocks. In other words, you already own the shares of stocks. Now, why would you want to write a call option on stocks you already own? The basis of this strategy is that you don't expect the stock price to move very much during the lifetime of the options contract, but you want to generate money over the short term in the form of premiums that you can collect. This can help you generate a short-term income stream; you must structure your calls carefully.

Setting up covered calls is relatively low risk and will help you get familiar with many of the aspects of options trading. While it's probably not going to make you rich overnight, it's a good way to learn the tools of the trade.

Covered Calls involve a long position

In order to create a covered call, you need to own at least 100 shares of stock in one underlying equity. When you create a call, you're going to be offering potential buyers a chance to buy these shares from you. Of course, the strategy is that you're only going to sell high, but your real goal is to get the income stream from the premium.

The premium is a one-time non-refundable fee. If a buyer purchases your call option and pays you the premium, that money is yours. No matter what happens after that, you've got that cash to keep. In the event that the stock doesn't reach the strike price, the contract will expire, and you can create a new call option on the same underlying shares. Of course, if the stock price does pass the strike price, the buyer of the contract will probably exercise their right to buy the shares. You will still earn money on the trade, but the risk is you're giving up the potential to earn as much money that could have been earned on the trade.

You write a covered call option that has a strike price of $67. Suppose that for some unforeseen reason the shares skyrocket to $90 a share. The buyer of your call option will be able to purchase the shares from you at $67. So, you've gained $2 a share. However, you've missed out on the chance to sell the shares at a profit of $35 a share. Instead, the investor who purchased the call option from you will turn around and sell the shares on the markets for the actual spot price and they will reap the benefits.

However, you really haven't lost anything. You have earned the premium plus sold your shares of stock for a modest profit.

That risk – that the stocks will rise to a price that is much higher than the strike price - always exists, but if you do your homework, you're going to be offering stocks that you don't expect to change much in price over the lifetime of your call. So, suppose instead that the price only rose to $68. The price exceeded the strike price so the buyer may exercise their option. In that case, you are still missing out on some profit that you could have had otherwise, but it's a small amount and we're not taking into account the premium.

In the event that the stock price doesn't exceed the strike price over the length of the contract, then you get to keep the premium and you get to keep the shares. The premium is yours to keep no matter what.

In reality, in most situations, a covered call is going to be a win-win situation for you.

Covered Calls are a Neutral Strategy

A covered call is known as a "neutral" strategy. Investors create covered calls for stocks in their portfolio where they only expect small moves over the lifetime of the contract. Moreover, investors will use covered calls on stocks that they expect to hold for the long term. It's a way to earn money on the stocks during a period in which the investor expects that the stock won't move much at price and so have no earning potential from selling.

An Example of a Covered Call

Let's say that you own 100 shares of Acme Communications. It's currently trading at $40 a share. Over the next several months, nobody is expecting the stock to move very much, but as an investor, you feel Acme Communications has solid long-term growth potential. To make a little bit of money, you sell a call option on Acme Communications with a strike price of $43. Suppose that the premium is $0.78 and that the call option lasts 3 months.

For 100 shares, you'll earn a total premium payment of $0.78 x 100 = $78. No matter what happens, you pocket the $78.

Now let's say that over the next three months the stock drops a bit in price so that it never comes close to the strike price, and at the end of the three-month period, it's trading at $39 a share.

The options contract will expire, and it's worthless. The buyer of the options contract ends up empty-handed. You have a win-win situation. You've earned the extra $78 per 100 shares, and you still own your shares at the end of the contract.

Now let's say that the stock does increase a bit in value. Over time, it jumps up to $42, and then to $42.75, but then drops down to $41.80 by the time the options contract expires. In this scenario, you're finding yourself in a much better position. In this case, the strike price of $43 was never reached, so the buyer of the call option is again left out in the cold. You, on the other hand, keep the premium of $78, and you still get to keep the shares of stock. This time since the shares have increased in value, you're a lot better off than you were before, so it's really a win-win situation for YOU, even though it's a losing situation for the poor soul who purchased your call.

Sadly, there is another possibility, that the stock price exceeds the strike price before the contract expires. In that case, you're required to sell the stock. You still end up in a position that isn't all that bad, however. You didn't lose any actual money, but you lost a potential profit. You still get the premium of $78, plus the earnings from the sale of the 100 shares at the strike price of $43.

A covered call is almost a zero-risk situation because you never actually lose money even though if the stock price soars, you obviously missed out on an opportunity. You can minimize that risk by choosing stocks you use for a covered call option carefully. For example, if you hold shares in a pharmaceutical company that is rumored to be announcing a cure for cancer in two months, you probably don't want to use those shares for a covered call. A company that has more long-term prospects but probably isn't going anywhere in the next few months is a better bet.

How to go about creating a covered call

To create a covered call, you'll need to own 100 shares of stock. While you don't want to risk a stock that is likely to take off in the near future, you don't want to pick a total dud either. There is always someone willing to buy something – at the right price. But you want to go with a decent stock so that you can earn a decent premium.

You start by getting online at your brokerage and looking up the stock online. When you look up stocks online, you'll be able to look at their "option chain" which will give you information from a table on premiums that are available for calls on this stock. You can see these listed under bid price. The bid price is given on a per share basis, but a call contract has 100 shares. If your bid price is $1.75, then the actual premium you're going to get is $1.75 x 100 = $175.

An important note is that the further out the expiration date, the higher the premium. A good rule of thumb is to pick an expiry that is between two and three months from the present date. Remember that the longer you go, the higher the risk because that increases the odds that the stock price will exceed the strike price and you'll end up having to sell the shares.

You have an option (no pun intended) with the premium you want to charge. Theoretically, you can set any price you want. Of course, that requires a buyer willing to pay that price for you to actually make the money. A more reasonable strategy is to look at prices people are currently requesting for call options on this stock. You can do this by checking the asking price for the call options on the stock. You can also see prices that buyers are currently offering by looking at the bid prices. For an instant sale, you can simply set your price to a bid price that is already out there. If you want to go a little bit higher, you can submit the order and then wait until someone comes along to buy your call option at the bid price.

To sell a covered call, you select "sell to open."

Benefits of Covered Calls

- A covered call is a relatively low-risk option. The worst-case scenario is that you'll be out of your shares but earn a small profit, a smaller profit than you could have made if you had not created the call contract and simply sold your shares. However, you also get the premium.
- A covered call allows you to generate income from your portfolio in the form of premiums.
- If you don't expect any price moves on the stock in the near term and you plan on holding it long term, it's a reasonable strategy to generate income without taking much risk.

Risks of Covered Calls

- Covered calls can be a risk if you're bullish on the stock, and your expectations are realized, and there is a price spike. In that case, you've traded the small amount of income of the premium with a voluntary cap of the strike price for the potential upside you could have had if you had simply held the stock and sold it at the high price.

- If the stock price plummets, while you still get the premium, the stocks will be worthless unless they rebound over the long term. You shouldn't use a call option on stocks that you expect to be on the path to a major drop in the coming months. In that case, rather than writing a covered call, you should simply sell the stocks and take your losses. Alternatively, you can continue holding the stocks to see if they rebound over the long term.

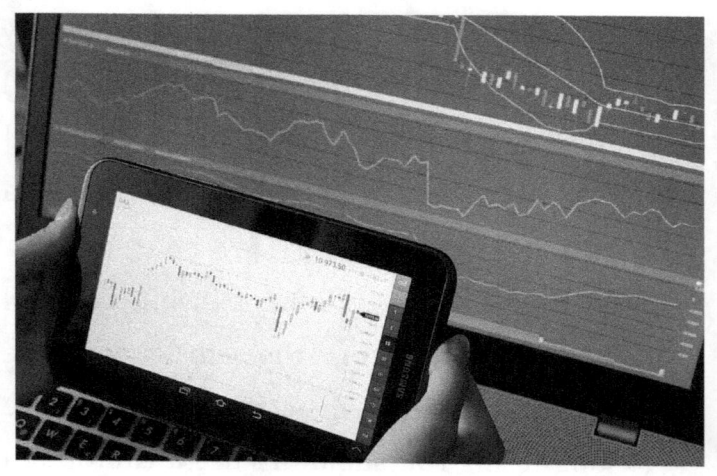

Chapter 7: Buying Calls

Buying calls is a more advanced form of training than selling covered calls. But it's not that complicated, so let's dive in.

What you're actually buying

Remember that one option contract is for 100 shares, so you'll need to be able to buy 100 shares of the stock in order to exercise your right to buy.

Also, remember that an options contract has a deadline. If the stock price fails to exceed the strike price by the deadline, you're out of luck and will lose whatever money that you invested in the premium. In relative terms, the premium price will be small so chances are if you are careful and not starting out by buying large numbers of options contracts, you won't be out that much money.

Your Goal Buying Options Contracts

The goal when purchasing options contracts is to buy a stock at a price that is lower than its current market value. In other words, you want the stock price to be significantly higher than the strike price so that you're enjoying significant savings in purchasing the stock. When evaluating your options, you'll need to take into account the added costs of the premium paid plus commissions. In some cases, commissions can be substantial so make sure you know what they are ahead of time so that you choose a good strike price and exercise your options at the right time.

You're a trader, not an investor

You may be mentally conditioned to think in terms of investing. An investor wants to build a diversified portfolio over a long time period that they believe will increase in value over the long term. A trader operates in the same universe but has different goals. You are after short term profits – not investments. You are not going to hold this stock. If you were interested in holding the stock, you would simply buy it at the lower price that is currently on offer. Your goal is to be able to buy at the strike price when the stock has increased significantly in price and then sell it immediately so that you can pocket the profits.

Let's take an example. Suppose that XYZ corporation is currently selling at $30 a share. People are expecting the stock to rise, and some people are really bullish about its short-term prospects. If you are an investor, your goal is to get the stock at the lowest possible price and then hold it long term. If you are using strategies like dollar cost averaging, you might be buying a few shares every month without paying too much attention to what the price is specifically on the day you purchase. In any case, as an investor, you'll simply buy the shares at $30.

As a trader, you're hoping to cash in on the moves of XYZ over the next couple of months. You'll buy an options contract, let's say its premium is $0.90 and the strike price is $35. Your cost for the 100 shares is $90.

Then the stock price shoots up to $45. Since it passed the strike price, you can exercise your option to buy the shares at the strike price. You can buy them at $35 for a total price of $3,500. But remember – you're not an investor in for the long haul. You'll immediately unload the shares. You sell the shares for $4,500 and make a $1,000 profit. After considering your premium, your profit is $910. It will go a little bit lower after considering commissions, but you get the idea. The purpose of buying call options is to make fast profits on stocks you think are going to spike.

It's hard to guess when the best time is to really buy call options. Obviously, you don't want to do it when a major recession hit. The optimal time is during a bull market, or when a specific company is expected to hit on something big, that will suddenly increase its value in the markets. A good time to look is also when a recession hits, but it passes the bottom out period.

Benefits of Buying Call Options

Call options have many benefits that we've already touched on earlier. In Particular:

- Call options allow you to control 100 shares of stock without actually investing in the 100 shares – unless they reach a price where you get the profit that you want.
- Call options allow you to sit and wait, patiently watching the market before making your move.
- If your bet doesn't work out, you're only going to lose a small amount of money on the contract. In our example, if XYZ loses value, and ends up at $28 per share instead

of moving past your strike price of $35, then you're only out the $90 you paid for the premium.

- Call buying provides a way to leverage expensive stock.

What to look for when buying Call options

Now let's take a look at some factors that you'll be on the lookout for when buying call options. You're going to want to be able to purchase shares of the stock you're interested in at a price that is less than the price you think it will go up to. You need to do this in order to ensure that the stock price surpasses the strike price. Of course, it's impossible to know what the future holds so this will involve a bit of speculation. You'll have to do a lot of reading and research to make educated guesses on where you expect the stock to go in the next few weeks or months.

Second, you'll need to take into account the cost of the premium when making your estimates. For the sake of simplicity, suppose that you find a call option with a premium of $1 per share. You're going to need a strike price that is high enough to take that into account. If you go for a stock that is $40 a share with a $1 premium and a strike price of $41, obviously you're not going to make anything unless the stock price goes higher than $41.

Remember that exercising your rights on the options contract is not a path toward immediate money. You're going to have to turn around and sell it ASAP in order to profit. Of course, when you sell is a judgment call as is when you exercise your right to buy. You're going to want to wait until the right moment to buy, but its impossible to really know what that right moment is. This is where trading experience helps and even then, the most skilled experts can make mistakes. For a beginner, the best thing to do is exercise your right to buy the shares and then sell them as soon as they've gone far enough past the strike price for you to make a profit and cover the premium. If you wait too long, there is always the chance that the stock price will start declining again, and it will go below your strike price and never exceed it again before the contract expires.

Open Interest

If you get online to check stocks you're interested in, one of the measures you will see is "Open Interest." This tells you the number of open or outstanding derivative contracts there are for that particular stock. Every time that a buyer and seller enter into an options contract, this value increases by one. What you want to do with open interest as a trader looking to make real cash from call options is to look for stocks that show big movement in the number of open trades. You're going to want to look for increasing numbers. This means that other traders have an interest in buying call options on this stock and that they're expecting it to go up in value in the near future.

Of course, you're going to want to take an educated approach to this. Simply getting online and going through random stocks will be a waste of time, it might take you weeks to find something.

You're going to want to prepare ahead of time by keeping an eye on the financial news. Watch Fox Business, read the Wall Street Journal, and watch CNBC and read any other financial publications that are to your liking. Find out what stocks the experts are talking about and which ones they expect to make significant moves over the next few weeks and months. Keep in mind these people and experts often make mistakes, so you're only using it as a guideline. You also don't want to focus solely on looking for stocks that are going to make moves; you want to keep up with company news. You need to keep your ears open for news such as the development of a new drug or the latest electronic gadget. Sometimes you might find out news about that before the stock begins attracting a lot of interest in the markets.

Tips for Buying Call Options

- Don't buy a call option with a strike price that you don't think the stock can beat.

- Always include the premium price in your analysis.

- Look for calls that are just in the money. These are likely to bring a modest profit.

- Call options that are out of the money might give you an option for a cheaper premium.

- However, the premium shouldn't be your primary consideration when looking to buy a call option. Compared to the money required to buy the shares and the potential profits if the stock goes past the strike price, the premium is going to be a trivial cost in most cases – provided of course the strike price is high enough to take the premium into account.

- Look at the time value. If you're looking for larger profits, it's better to aim for longer contracts. Remember, that with any call option you have the option to buy the stock at the strike price at any time between today's date and the deadline when the stock market price exceeds the strike price. Longer time frames mean you increase the chances of that happening. Even if the price goes a little above the strike price and dips down, with a longer window of time before the deadline, you can wait and see if it rebounds. Remember if it never does, you're only out the premium.

- Start small. Beginning traders shouldn't bet the farm on options. You'll end up broke if you do that. The better approach is to start by investing in one contract at a time and gaining experience as you go.

Chapter 8: Volatility in the Markets

While the stock market has long term trends that investors rely on fairly well as the years and decades go by, over the short term the stock market is highly volatile. By that, we mean that prices are fluctuating up and down and doing so over short time periods. Volatility is something that long-term investors ignore. It's why you will hear people that promote conservative investment strategies suggesting that buyers use dollar cost averaging. What this does is it averages out the volatility in the market. That way you don't risk making the mistake of buying stocks when the price is a bit higher than it should be, because you'll average that out by buying shares when it's a bit lower than it should be.

In a sense, over the short term, the stock market can be considered as a chaotic system. So from one day to the next, unless there is something specific on offer, like Apple introducing a new gadget that investors are going to think will be a major hit, you can't be sure what the stock price is going to be tomorrow or the day after that. An increase on one day doesn't mean more increases are coming; it might be followed by a major dip the following day.

For example, at the time of writing, checking Apple's stock price, on the previous Friday it bottomed out at $196. Over the following days, it went up and down several times, and on the most recent close, it was $203. The movements over a short-term period appear random, and to a certain extent, they are. It's only over the long term that we see the actual direction that Apple is heading.

Of course, Apple is at the end of a ten-year run that began with the introduction of the iPhone and iPad. It's a reasonable bet that while it's a solid long-term investment, the stock probably isn't going to be moving enough for the purposes of making good profits over the short term from trades on call options (not too mention the per share price is relatively high).

The truth is volatility is actually a friend of the trader who buys call options. But it's a friend you have to be wary of because you can benefit from volatility while also getting in big trouble from it.

The reason stocks with more volatility are the friend of the options trader is that in part the options trader is playing a probability game. In other words, you're looking for stocks that have a chance of beating the strike price you need in order to make profits. A volatile stock that has large movements has a greater probability of not only passing your strike price but doing so in such a fashion that it far exceeds your strike price enabling you to make a large profit.

Of course, the alternative problem exists – that the stock price will suddenly drop. That is why care needs to be a part of your trader's toolkit. A stock with a high level of volatility is just as likely to suddenly drop in price as it is to skip right past your strike price.

Moreover, while you're a beginner and might get caught with your pants down, volatile stocks are going to attract experienced options traders. That means that the stock will be in high demand when it comes to options contracts. What happens when there is a high demand for something? The price shoots up. In the case of call options, that means the stock will come with a higher premium. You will need to take the higher premium into account when being able to exercise your options at the right time and make sure the price is high enough above your strike price that you don't end up losing money.

Traders take some time to examine the volatility of a given stock over the recent past, but they also look into what's known as implied volatility. This is a kind of weather forecast for stocks. It's an estimate of the future price movements of a stock, and it has a large influence on the pricing of options. Implied volatility is denoted by the Greek symbol **σ,** implied volatility increases in bear markets, and it actually decreases when investors are bullish. Implied volatility is a tool that can provide insight into the options future value.

For options traders, more volatility is a good thing. A stock that doesn't have much volatility is going to be a stable stock whose price isn't going to change very much over the lifetime of a contract. So while you may want to sell a covered call for a stock with low volatility, you're probably not going to want to buy one if you're buying call options because that means there will be a lower probability that the stock will change enough to exceed the strike price so you can earn a profit on a trade. Remember too that stocks that are very volatile will attract a lot of interest from options traders and command higher premiums. You will have to do some balancing in picking stocks that are of interest.

Being able to pick stocks that will have the right amount of volatility so that you can be sure of getting one that will earn profits on short term trades is something you're only going to get from experience. You should spend some time practicing before actually investing large amounts of money. That is, pick stocks you are interested in and make your bets but don't actually make the trades. Then follow them over the time period of the contract and see what happens. In the meantime, you can purchase safer call options, and so using this two-pronged approach gain experience that will lead to more surefire success down the road.

One thing that volatility means for everyone is that predicting the future is an impossible exercise. You're going to have some misses no matter how much knowledge and experience you gain. The only thing to aim for is to beat the market more often than you lose. The biggest mistake you can make is putting your life savings into a single stock that you think is a sure thing and then losing it all.

Options to pursue if your options aren't working

At this point, you may think that if the underlying stock for your option doesn't go anywhere or it tanks that you have no choice but to wait out the expiration date and count the money you spend on your premiums as a loss. That really isn't the case. The truth is, you can sell a call option you've purchased to other traders in the event its not working for you. Of course, you're not going to make a profit taking this approach in the vast majority of cases. But it will give you a chance to recoup some of your losses. If you have invested in a large number of call options for a specific stock and it's causing you problems, you need to recoup at least some of your losses may be more acute. Of course, the right course of action in these cases is rarely certain, especially if the expiration date for the contract is relatively far off in the future, which could mean that the stock has many chances to turn around and beat your strike price. Remember, in all bad scenarios actually buying the shares of stock is an option – you're not required to do it. In all cases, the biggest loss you're facing is losing the entire premium. You'll also want to keep the following rule of thumb in mind at all times – the more time value an option has, the higher the price you can sell the option for. If there isn't much time value left, then you're probably going to have to sell the option at a discount. If there is a lot of time value, you may be able to recoup most of your losses on the premium.

Let's look at some specific scenarios.

- The stock is languishing. If the stock is losing time value (that is getting closer to the expiration date) and doesn't seem to be going anywhere, you can consider selling the call option in order to recoup some of your losses related to the premium. The more time value, the less likely it is that selling the option is a good idea. Of course, the less time value, the harder it's going to be to actually sell your option. Or put another way, in order to actually sell it you're going to have to take a lower price.

- Suppose the stock isn't stagnant, but it's tanking. If there is a lot of time value left *and* there is some reason to believe that the company is going to make moves before the expiration date of your contract that will improve the fortunes of the stock when you can still profit from it, then you may want to ride out the downturn. This is a risky judgment call, and it's going to be impossible to know for sure what the right answer is, but you can make an educated guess. On the other hand, if the stock is tanking and there is no good news about the company on the horizon, you are pretty much facing the certainty that you're not going to be able to exercise your options to buy the shares. In that case, you should probably look at selling the option contract to someone more willing to take the risk. At least you can get some of the money back that you paid for the premium.

Now let's briefly consider the positive scenario. Buying options and then trading the stocks can feel like a roller coaster ride, and that rush is what attracts a lot of people to options trading besides the possibilities of making short term profits. Let's consider an example where the stock keeps rising in price? How long do you wait before selling?

There are two risks here. The first risk is that you're too anxious to sell and so do it at the first opportunity. That really isn't a huge downside; you're going to make some profits in that case. On the other hand, it's going to be disconcerting when you sit back and watch the stock continuing to rise. That said, this is better than some of the alternatives.

One of the alternatives is waiting too long to buy and sell the shares. You might wait and see the stock apparently reaching a peak, and then get a little greedy hoping that it's going to keep increasing so you can make even more profits. But then you keep waiting, and suddenly the stock starts dropping. Maybe you wait a little more hoping it's going to start rebounding and going up again, but it doesn't, and you're forced to buy and sell at a lower price than you could have gotten. Maybe it's even dropping enough so that you lose your opportunity altogether. A really volatile stock might suddenly crash, leaving you with a lost opportunity.

The reality is that like everything else involved in options trading since none of us can see the future it's going to be flat out impossible to know if you are making the right call every single time. Keep in mind that your goal is to make a profit on your trades. Don't get greedy about it, hoping for more riches than you actually see on the screen. In other words, the goal isn't to sell at maximum possible profits. Nobody knows what those are because it's going to be virtually impossible to predict what price the stock will peak at before the contract expires. Instead, you're going to want to focus on making an acceptable profit. Before you even buy your call options, you should sit down and figure out a reasonable range of values that define ahead of time what that acceptable profit level is. Then when the stock price hits your target range, you exercise your options and sell the shares. You take your profit and move on, going to the next trades.

That is not a guarantee that you're going to make money on every trade, but it's a more rules-based system that gets you into the mindset of trading based on objective facts rather than relying on unbridled emotions.

Also, remember that you can exercise the option to buy the shares, and then hold them until you think you've reached the right moment to sell. At other times, you may want to exercise the option to buy shares and hold in your portfolio as a long-term investment.

Chapter 9: In the money, out of the money

When trading options you're often going to hear the terms in the money and out of the money. We've defined them but lets briefly take a closer look at what they mean.

In the Money

In the money simply means that exercising the option would result in a profit. For a call option, that means that the current stock price has risen above the strike price.

If Acme Communications is trading at $100 a share, and you have a call option with a strike price of $60, that means that you're in the money and you can buy the shares at $60 and sell them for $100 in the market. The option contract is said to have an intrinsic value that is equal to the difference between the stock price and the strike price, that is $100-$60 = 40 is the intrinsic value.

When you automatically exercise your options

If you have enough cash in your brokerage account when the call option contract expires to cover the purchase of the underlying shares at the strike price, if the call option expires in the money, then you're going to purchase the stocks automatically. Of course, you can sell them right away for a profit or hold them, your choice at that point.

Out of the Money

When the strike price is higher than the market price of the underlying asset, the call option is said to be out of the money. A call option that is out of the money has no intrinsic value, but it may have time value. Any option that reaches the expiry is worthless if it's out of the money at that point. However, if it still has time value and the underlying asset has been increasing in value such that the option is closer to being in the money, then it may be valuable enough to sell the option to another investor, and they may purchase it from you at a higher price than you paid for the premium. So, remember here that we are talking about trading the option itself, and not the underlying stock. So if you sell the option to someone else, you may recoup all or part of the premium, or even make a profit on it, however, the investor who buys it from you will be the one who can exercise the right to buy the stocks and/or hold the option until the expiration date.

Chapter 10: Buying and Selling Puts

So far, we've talked exclusively about buying and selling call options. Generally speaking, this is a better option for beginning traders. Our belief is that starting out selling covered call options, then moving on to limited purchases of call options is the best way to get started in options trading. Once you gain experience in that, you can move on to trading options themselves and also with buying and selling put options.

Let's quickly review what's involved in puts. A put is a bet on a decrease in stock price. Truthfully, puts aren't really all that different than calls, because a call is based on an educated hunch that some stock is going to go up in price in the coming weeks or months. A put is a bet that the opposite will occur, in other words, that the stock market price is going to decrease in the coming weeks or months.

First, let's look at how in-the-money and out-of-the-money are defined for puts.

How a Put Option Works

A put option from the buyer's perspective is the option to sell the underlying stock asset at a pre-agreed strike price. In this case, the bet you're making as the buyer of the contract is that the stock price is going to drop in value, and then you can sell the shares to the seller of the put contract at a higher price.

Suppose there is a pharmaceutical company called Theran Nose. Let's say that the shares are currently trading at $100, but there is bad news swirling around. You've studied the situation and are confident the stock will fall and do so more than dropping to $70. You find a seller of a put contract that doesn't think it's going to drop that much by the expiration date, and so they sell you the put option with a $70 strike price.

Then a week before the expiration date, the price crashes to $40 a share. In the case of a put, the seller of the put MUST purchase the shares from you. So, you buy the stock at $40 a share, and then you sell the shares to the seller at $70 a share. Needless to say, they will be seriously irritated, but you made a better bet and come out with a profit of $30 a share.

In the Money

In the case of a put option, when the stock price is below the strike price, it is said to be in the money. If the strike price is $150, and the stock price is $100, the put option has an intrinsic value of $50. The buyer of the put can buy the stock at $100 a share and sell it for $150 a share.

Out of the money

In the case of a put, if the market price is above the strike price, then there is no intrinsic value. In an analogous fashion to that we've seen for call options, however, if the contract has time value, then it may still be possible to profit from the contract. You may be able to sell it to another investor and get some or all of your premium back, or if there is enough time value, and it looks like even though the stock has yet to decline below the strike price that there are decent odds that it will, then you might get lucky and find an investor who will buy the option contract from you.

Using Puts as Insurance

So far, we've talked about put options in terms of speculating. That is, over the short-term interval of the contract, you believe that the underlying stock is going to drop in price and do so by dropping below the strike price. However, a put option can also be used as a form of insurance for securities in your portfolio. This can work for index funds or for individual stocks.

Suppose you have a stock that you're hoping to hold for the long term. Its prospects are uncertain, so there is a chance that you could lose a lot of money. Maybe you've invested in 1,000 shares. If you do nothing and the stock tanks, then you're out of luck. For the sake of example, we'll say that you bought the stock at $10 a share, for a total price of $10,000. Then after some bad news, it tanks, dropping to $2 a share. Now you're left with an investment worth just $2,000, and you lost $8,000. Your only hope is to either sell now and cut your losses or hold it and hope that things get better in the future.

Another alternative is to buy some put contracts on the stock. Let's say the contracts have a premium of $0.56, so it costs $56 to buy a put contract for 100 shares. Altogether, you'll have to invest $560 to buy enough to cover your entire investment.

Now suppose that they came with a strike price of $7.

The stock tanks to $2 a share. You can then sell your shares at $7 to the seller of the puts. That gives you $7,000 back. Incorporating the cost of the premium, you've recovered $6,440.

Although you haven't recovered all of your losses, it's certainly true that having $6,440 is far better than only being able to recoup $2,000. We see how a put acting as an insurance policy can help protect our existing investments.

Speculating with Puts

Speculating with puts is trickier than doing so with call options. In fact, the most famous options traders are those who "short" a stock, and there is a good reason. Knowing which stocks are going to fall might seem obvious, but it doesn't always work that way. Without getting inside information, which of course is illegal, you're going to have to make educated guesses. In other words, the advice here is basically the same as it is with calls. You'll have to study the markets and watch all the financial news networks to find out what companies have prospects for heading into a downturn. Overall, of course, a bear market or recession will be the best time to look for a prospect for put options.

Chapter 11: Beginners Common Mistakes

Trading options are more involved than trading stocks, so there are ample opportunities to make mistakes. It's important to take the approach of going small and slow at first so that you don't lose the shirt off your back. That said, if you run into mistakes don't get too down about it. Dust yourself off and get up to fight another day. With that said, let's have a look at some common mistakes and how to avoid them.

Putting all your eggs in one basket
While there is a difference between investing and trading, as traders can learn a few things from our investor brothers (and most people are a little of both anyway). Don't let everything ride on one trade. If you take all the money you have and invest it in buying options for one stock, you're making a big mistake. Doing that is very risky, and as a beginning trader, you're going to want to mitigate your risk as much as possible. Betting on

one stock may pay off sometimes, but more times than not it's going to lead you into bankruptcy territory.

Investing more than you can

It's easy to get excited about options trading. The chances to make fast money and the requirements that you analyze the markets can be very enticing. Oftentimes that leads people into getting more excited than they should. A good rule to follow with investing is to make sure that you're setting aside enough money to cover living expenses every month, with a security fund for emergencies. Don't bet the farm on some sure thing by convincing yourself that you'll be able to make back twice as much money and so cover your expenses. Things don't always work out.

Going all in before you're ready

Another mistake is failing to take the time to learn options trading in real time. Just like getting overly excited can cause people to bet too much money or put all their money on one stock, some people are impatient and don't want to take the time to learn the options markets by selling covered calls. It's best to start with covered calls and then move slowly to small deals buying call options. Leave put options until you've gained some experience.

Failure to study the markets

Remember, you need to be truly educated to make good options trades. That means you'll need to know a lot about the companies that you're either trying to profit from or that you're shorting. Options trading isn't possible without some level of guesswork, but make your guesses educated guesses, and don't rely too much on hunches.

Not Getting Enough Time Value

Oftentimes, whether you're trading puts or calls, the time value is important. A stock may need an adequate window of time in order to beat the stock price whether it's going above it or plunging below it. When you're starting out and don't know the markets as well as a seasoned trader, you should stick to options you can buy that have a longer time period before expiring.

Not having adequate liquidity

Sometimes beginning investors overestimate their ability to play the options markets. Remember that if you buy an option, to make it work for you- you're going to need money on hand to buy stocks when the iron is hot. And you're going to need to buy 100 shares for every option contract. Before entering into the contract, make sure that you're going to be able to exercise your option.

Not having a grip on volatility

If you don't understand volatility and its relation to premium pricing, you may end up making bad trades.

Failing to have a plan

Trading seems exciting, and when you're trading, you may lose the investors mentality. However, traders need to have a strategic plan as much as investors do. Before trading, make sure that you have everything in place, including knowing what your goals are for the trades, having pre-planned exit strategies, developing criteria for getting into a trade so that you're not doing on a whim or based on emotion.

Ignoring Expiration Dates

It sounds crazy, but many beginners don't keep track of the expiration date. Would you hate to see a stock go up in price, and then hope it keeps going up, and it does, only to find out that your expiration date passed before you exercised your option?

Overleveraging

It's easy to spend huge amounts of money in small increments. This is true when it comes to trading options. Since stocks are more expensive, it's possible to get seduced by purchasing low priced options. After all, options are available at a fraction of the cost that is required to buy stocks. And you might keep on purchasing them until you're overleveraged.

Buying cheap options

In many cases, buying cheap things isn't a good strategy. If you're buying a used car, while you might occasionally find a great car that is a good buy, in most cases a car is cheap for a reason. The same applies to options trading. When it comes to options, a cheap premium probably denotes the option is out of the money. Sure, you save some money on a cheap premium, but when the expiration date comes, you might see the real reason the option contract was a cheap buy. Of course, as we described earlier, there may be cases where cheap options have the capacity to rebound and become profitable by the time the expiry date arrives. But taking chances like that is best left to experienced traders.

Giving in to panic

Remember that you have the right to buy or sell a stock if you've purchased an option. Some beginners panic and exercise their right far too early. This can happen because of fears that they'll be missing out an opportunity with a call option, or because of fears that a stock won't keep going down on a put.

Not Knowing how much cash you can afford to lose

Going into options trading blindly is not a smart move. With each option trade you make, you need to have a clear idea of how much cash you have on hand to cover losses and exercising your options. You'll also want to know how much cash you can afford to lose if things go south.

Jumping into puts without enough experience and cash to cover losses

Remember if you're selling puts, you will have to buy the stock at the strike price if the buyer exercises their option. This is a huge risk. The stock could have plunged in value, and you're going to have to buy the stock at the strike price, possibly leaving you with huge losses. Don't go into selling puts with your eyes closed, in fact, beginners are better off avoiding selling puts. But if you must do it, make sure you can absorb the losses when you bet wrong.

Piling it on

Most beginner mistakes are related to panic. If you're looking at losses on options, some beginners double and triple up hoping to make it up when things turn better. Instead, they end up losing more money. Instead of giving in to panic, learn when to cut your losses and re-evaluate your trading strategy.

Staying in a written contract when you should get out

If you've sold an option and it's looking like you might face a loss, you can always get out of it by selling.

Chapter 12: Advanced Trading Strategies

In this chapter, we'll look at some advanced trading strategies.

Long Straddle

In a long straddle, you'll simultaneously buy a put and call for the same underlying stock. You're also going to want the same strike price and expiration date. This technique is something that can be utilized with a highly volatile stock. That way you have the possibility of profiting no matter which way the stock moves. Before we see how this works, let's step back for a second and recall how we determine whether or not a deal is going to be profitable. We are looking at this from the buyer's perspective.

In a call option, you're going to profit when the stock exceeds the strike price. However, you must remember to include the premium in your calculation. If you think a stock will go higher than $54, but you're paying a $1 premium per share, then you will have to invest in a call option that has a strike price of at least $55.

In a put option, it's the same game, but you're hoping the stock will go below the strike price. So, for our new scenario of buying a call and a put at the same strike price and expiration date, we will buy a put with a strike price of $55. For simplicity, we will stay with a $1 premium.

Now you need to know the net premium, which will be the sum of the premium from the call option + the premium from the put option, in this case, $2.

You can get a profit when one of two conditions are met:

- Price of underlying stock > (Strike price of call + Net Premium). In our example, you will make a profit when the amount of the underlying stock is higher than $55 + $2 = $57.

- Price of underlying stock < (Strike price of put – Net Premium). Using our example, you'll see a profit when the price of the underlying stock is less than $55- $2 = $53.

The maximum loss for a straddle will occur when the contract expires with the underlying trading at the strike price. In that case, both contracts expire, and you're out the premiums paid for both options.

A long straddle has two break-even points. These are:

- Lower breakeven point: Strike price – Net premium
- Upper breakeven point: Strike price + Net premium

Remember you buy both options with the same strike price and expiration date.

Let's look at a simple example. A stock is trading at $100 a share in May. The investor buys a call with a strike price of $200 that expires on the third Friday in June for $100. The investor also buys a put with a strike price of $200 that expires on the third Friday of June for $100.

The net premium is $100 + $100 = $200.

Now suppose that on the expiry date, the stock is trading at $300. The put expires as worthless since the stock price of the underlying is far above the strike price of the put. However, the investor's call option expires in the money with an intrinsic value of 100 x ($300 - $200) = $10,000. Less the premium the investor has made $9,800.

On the other hand, suppose that the stock drops in value, and on the expiry is trading at $50. This time, the call option expires as worthless. The investor can buy 100 shares at a price of $50 each for a total cost of $5,000. Now he can sell them to exercise the put option at $200 a share, so he nets $20,000 - $5,000 - $200 = $14,800.

This is a fictitious example, so whether the numbers are realistic or not really isn't the point – the point is that the investor will profit no matter what happens to the stock price.

Strangle

The term strangle is an adaptation of the straddle. In this case, you also simultaneously buy a call option and a put option. However, instead of buying them at the same strike price, you buy them at different strike prices. For this type of strategy, you will buy slightly out-of-money options. This is used when you think that the underlying stock will undergo significant volatility in the short term. You will achieve a profit with a strangle when one of two conditions are met:

- Price of underlying stock > (strike price of call + Net Premium paid) or
- Price of underlying stock < (strike price of put – Net premium paid)

Usually, the strike price of the put is set at a lower value. Profit is determined by one of two possibilities:

- Profit = Price of underlying stock – strike price of call – net premium
- Profit = Strike price of put– the price of underlying stock – net premium

Bear Spread

A bear spread is profitable when the underlying stock price declines. Like the above strategies, a bear spread involves the simultaneous purchase of more than one option; however, in a bear spread, you buy two options of the same type. Alternatively, a call bear spread involves selling a call with a low strike price and buying a call with a high strike price.

Bull Spread

A bull spread is designed to profit when the price of the underlying security has a modest price increase. You can do a bull spread using either call or put options.

Married Puts

A married put is basically an insurance policy like that we described earlier. You buy a stock and a put option at the same time, in order to protect yourself against possible losses from the stock.

Cash Secured Puts

In a cash-secured put, you secure the possible purchase of stock by having money in your brokerage account to cover the purchase. This will allow you to purchase stock at a discount, provided you have enough money in your account to actually buy the stock. In short, you write a put option and set aside the cash to purchase the stock. Cash secured put is done when you are bullish on the underlying stock but believe it will undergo a temporary downturn.

Rolling

Rolling a trade simply means that you are simultaneously closing out your existing positions and opening new ones based on the same underlying stock. When rolling a position, you can change the strike price, the duration of the contract, or both. You can roll forward, which means to extend the expiration date for the option.

A roll-up means that you increase the strike price when you open the new contract. A roll-up is used on a call option when you believe the underlying stock is going to increase in price. When you are trading put options, you use a roll down. In that case, you close your option and reopen it with the same underlying stock but with a lower strike price. A higher strike price means that the new position will be cheaper. When rolling, you're going out in time to deadline. When rolling a call, you're hoping that the stock will rise in price. In this case, you're rolling to an out of the money position. The price of the new call will drop. With a put, the opposite occurs, and the price of the new put will increase.

Conclusion

Thank you for taking the time to read this book. If you have found this book useful as a tool for your investment education, please take a moment to jump on Amazon and offer an honest review. We sincerely hope that the information contained herein will help you grow and learn how to invest more wisely and realize greater profits.

Many investors are struck with fear at the mere mention of options trading. Derivatives are a mysterious concept that harkens visions of the 2008 financial collapse. This is the kind of brainwashing that we constantly receive from financial experts (who don't want you intruding on their secret games) and from friends, family, and media, who have left us conditioned so that we are too risk averse. The fact is if you understand the markets, options trading is not nearly as dangerous as it's made out to be. Moreover, it's far more exciting and interesting than taking the completely safe and boring path, investing in mutual funds or just letting the money sit inside your 401k.

While this book certainly does not cover everything, you need to know about options, as it's an introductory book that only scratches the surface, you have enough foundational knowledge to begin your foray into the world of options trading. We hope that you will approach your trading activities sensibly. This means that while you're going to be more willing to assume risk than someone locked into mutual funds, or simply buying and holding stocks from the stock market, that you will still take a reasonable and conservative approach to trade. We advise new traders to start slowly, focusing on one type of trade and growing as they gain experience and confidence. Stay conservative as you begin by writing call options for stocks that you already own so that you can benefit from the premium income while not taking much real risk. If you follow this path, even if you do end up losing your shares, you'll do so at a modest profit. That gives you the opportunity to load up and do it again and keep repeating the process until you've achieved mastery. As you gain experience, then you'll be able to move on to more ambitious types of trading and hopefully larger profits.

The first time that you start seeing profits rolling in from your options trading, you'll feel a tinge of excitement that let's be honest – few people actually experience these days. Remember to review not only the best techniques used but go over the beginner's mistakes so that you'll reduce the chances that you'll be the person making them. And most importantly, please remember that this book is only a starting point. You'll want to read my other books and also use them as a springboard to more advanced and detailed treatments. Best of luck and many profits in your trading activities!